A Word About
Soccer

BRIMAX

What to wear

Every soccer team has its own special 'strip' to wear. The colour and style of their top, shorts and socks is what identifies a team on the pitch.

shorts

long-sleeved shirt

short-sleeved shirt

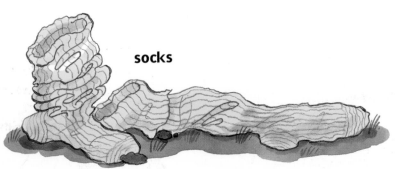

socks

Boots

moulded studs

Modern soccer boots are designed to be flexible and supple. Some boots have moulded studs on their base, which are most suitable for dry pitch conditions.

interchangeable studs

Some boots have screw-in studs. This means that different types of studs can be worn on the boots depending on whether the ground is hard, soft, or wet and slippery.

Astroturf boots

Modified training shoes called Astroturf boots are usually worn when playing on artificial grass pitches. These boots give better grip on hard surfaces and also cushion the feet.

To protect your legs you should also wear shinguards. These are worn underneath the socks.

Who's in a team?

Soccer is a team sport where players try to score goals by passing and dribbling a ball across a pitch, and then kicking or heading it into the opposing team's goal. Apart from the goalkeeper, and when taking throw-ins, players are not allowed to touch the ball with their hands or arms. There are normally eleven players in a soccer team.

goalkeeper

A goalkeeper has to stop his opponents from putting the ball into his goal. The goalkeeper is the only player allowed to handle the ball.

striker

A striker's job is to put the ball into the back of the net. A good striker has to have the ability and speed to move away from his opponents and score.

midfield player

Midfield players need lots of energy because they have to run around a lot. When attacking they move the ball up the pitch and try to pass to a team member who can score.

defender

A defender's main job is to prevent the other team's players from having a chance to score. They do this by marking attacking players and putting them under pressure.

Each member of a soccer team plays mainly in a 'third' of the pitch depending on what type of player they are. The third of the pitch closest to a player's own goal is their team's 'defending third'. The middle third of the pitch is called 'midfield'. The third of the pitch closest to the opponents' goal is a team's 'attacking third'.

Soccer skills

Soccer players need to have excellent ball skills. Keeping control of the ball is very important. Players must also be able to perform trick shots or moves to surprise their opponents.

chest pass

Soccer players can use their chests to redirect a ball to another player by quickly turning left or right.

header

Timing and good position are important when making a header.

backheel pass

A backheel pass can be made with the heel or the sole of the foot.

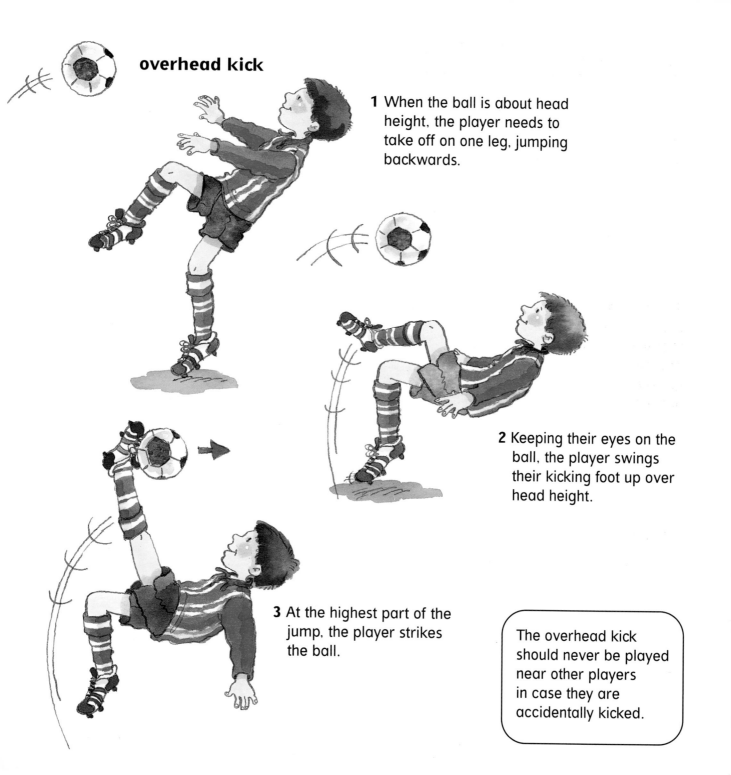

overhead kick

1 When the ball is about head height, the player needs to take off on one leg, jumping backwards.

2 Keeping their eyes on the ball, the player swings their kicking foot up over head height.

3 At the highest part of the jump, the player strikes the ball.

The overhead kick should never be played near other players in case they are accidentally kicked.

corner flagpost

goal area

centre mark

penalty arc

goal line

touch line

half way line

corner arc

penalty area

centre circle

penalty spot

goal

On the pitch

White marker paint is used to mark out different areas on the pitch.

centre mark

The centre mark is the point from which the game kicks-off.

touch line

A throw-in happens when the ball crosses the touchline. The throw is taken from the spot at which the ball crossed the line and by the team who did not put the ball out of play.

penalty spot

The ball is placed on the penalty spot for a penalty kick. A penalty can be given if the defending team foul in their own penalty area. When a penalty is being taken, all the other players must stand outside the penalty area until the ball is kicked.

corner arc

When the ball crosses the goal line and was last touched by a member of the defending team, a corner kick is given. The ball is placed inside the corner arc and kicked into the penalty area to the player who is in the best position to score.

Field formations

A formation is the basic shape of a soccer team on the pitch. Each team can arrange its defenders, midfield and attacking players in a variety of ways.

four-four-two

4-3-3 is a more attacking formation. The three strikers spread across the pitch to attack the goal, whilst midfielders protect defense.

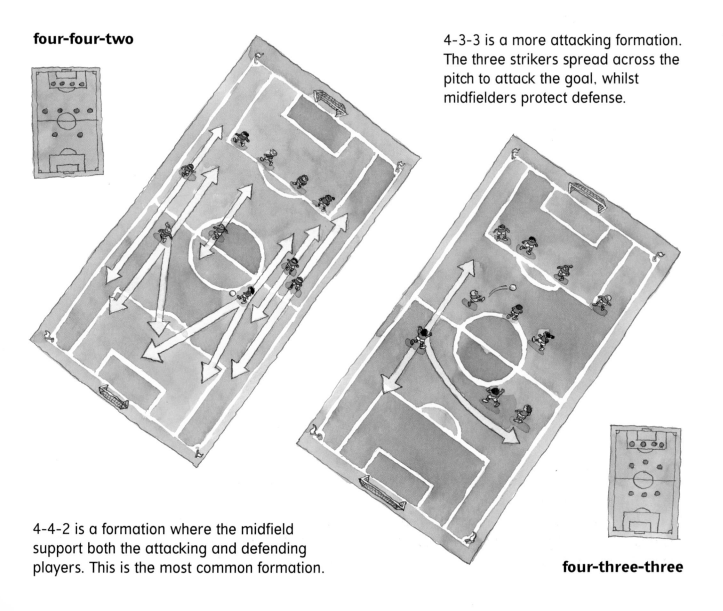

4-4-2 is a formation where the midfield support both the attacking and defending players. This is the most common formation.

four-three-three

Blowing the whistle

There are many strict rules to follow in professional soccer. The referee is on the pitch to make sure the players in each team obey and stick to the rules during a match.

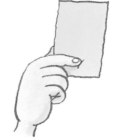

yellow card

The referee holds up a yellow card to show when a player has been cautioned.

whistle

The referee starts and stops play by blowing his whistle.

red card

A red card is used by the referee when a player is 'sent off'.

referee

the off-side rule

The referee also blows his whiste when a player is off-side. A player is off-side if he is closer to his opponent's goal-line than the ball at the moment it is passed to them, unless there are two or more opposition players at least as close to their goal line.

linesmen

To assist the referee, two linesmen watch the game from opposite sides of the pitch.

linesman's flag

If a player breaks the rules, or if the ball goes out of play, linesmen use flags to signal this.

keeping time

Two 'halves' of 45 minutes each are played in a match. The referee will add on 'extra time' if the game has been delayed by injury.

Practising at home

Every soccer player needs to practise. Here are some exercises recommended by the top players and coaches to help improve your ball control and fitness.

keeping the ball in the air

The idea of this exercise is to keep the ball in the air for as long as possible without letting it touch the ground. You can use your feet, your thighs or your head to control the ball and keep it in the air. You can also bounce the ball on your head and foot alternately.

Don't forget to 'warm up' before you begin any exercises. Swing your arms, twist your hips and jog on the spot.

Once you can control the ball with your feet, thighs and head, try linking all the exercises together – foot, thigh, head, thigh, foot.

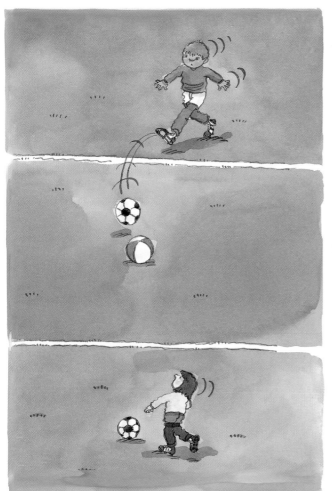

following the leader

This exercise is for two or more players. Choose one person to be the leader – this person dribbles the ball. Now line up behind the leader and follow every move they make. The leader must make lots of turns, stops and changes of speed. After a minute, the leader must pass the ball backwards and then join the back of the line.

target practice

This exercise is for two players. Divide an area into three 'thirds'. The two players face each other in the two 'thirds' which are furthest apart. Each player has a ball. An unusual coloured ball, the target, is placed in the centre of the middle third. Each player must try to move this 'target' across the other players' line and into their area by striking it with their own ball.

Glossary

challenge a direct attempt to get the ball back from an opponent.

chip a kick which makes the ball rise quickly into the air.

dead ball when a ball is out of play.

downfield kicking the ball towards your own goal.

dribbling a way for players to move the ball up the pitch, keeping it close to their foot as they run.

free kick given to the opposition when a foul is committed outside the penalty area.

goal a net structure at either end of the pitch, used to kick the soccer ball into to score a goal.

goalkeeper member of a soccer team who guards his team's goal.

formation the basic shape of a soccer team on the pitch.

jockeying delaying the opponent's attack by getting in their way.

strip style and colour of the clothing worn by soccer teams. Each soccer 'strip' is unique to a team and identifies players on the pitch.

penalty when a player commits a serious offence inside his own penalty area, the referee awards the attacking team a 'penalty' kick.

referee an official who controls a soccer match and makes the decision when to stop and restart play.

squad a group name for all the team members who play in each match.

substitutes extra players who wait on the sidelines of the pitch and who are asked to play if another player is injured.

team the eleven members needed on each side to play in a match.

upfield kicking the ball towards the opponents goal.

volleying kicking the ball before it has hit the ground.

wings the edges of the pitch along either touchline.